Alma y Corazón

WRITING IN THE RHYTHM OF LIFE

Poetry by Lupe Castillo and Teresa Ortiz
Drawings by Aaron Johnson-Ortiz

Flexible Press
Minneapolis, Minnesota, 2026

COPYRIGHT © 2026 Lupe Castillo, Teresa Ortiz,
and Aaron Johnson-Ortiz

All Rights Reserved. This is a work of poetry and art.
Names, characters, places, and incidents are the products of the author's imagination, and any resemblance to an actual person, living or dead, events, or locales is entirely coincidental.
No reproduction or quotation is permitted without the express permission of the authors/creators.

Print ISBN: 979-8-9998771-0-9

Flexible Press LLC
Minneapolis, Minnesota
www.flexiblepub.com

Cover art, "Estratigrafia Mexicana," by Aaron Johnson-Ortiz
Editor William E Burleson

Poetry by Lupe Castillo and Teresa Ortiz

PREFACE 4

POEMS BY LUPE CASTILLO
    IDENTITY 9
    FAMILIA 16
    SPIRITUAL 24
    ACTIVISM 38
    LOVE 47
    EARTH 51

POEMS BY TERESA ORTIZ
    IDENTITY 61
    FAMILIA 67
    EARTH 78
    ACTIVISM 86
    SPIRITUAL 100

ACKNOWLEDGMENTS 116
ABOUT THE ARTISTS 118

Alma Y Corazón

WRITING IN THE RHYTHM OF LIFE

To my beloved daughter and son, Carmen Maya and Aaron Marley.
To the loving memory of my Angel in Heaven, Gabriel Dominic.
To young Latina poets and artists, illuminating our lives with beauty and joy.

— Teresa Ortiz

This poetry book is dedicated to the spirit of my ancestors, Mi Reina Abuelita, Micaela, for loving me unconditionally, and to my children and grandchildren who carry our legacy into our future and our stories in their hearts. To aspiring writers and poets, you are seen as we bear witness to your stories.

—Lupe Castillo

Preface

In early 2000, Lupe Castillo and Teresa Ortiz were invited to be part of a new group of Latino spoken-word writers who would later be called Palabristas. When Teresa and Lupe met, they quickly realized that they both shared a love for family, community, and poetry.

At that time, Teresa Ortiz was working at the Resource Center of the Americas, on Minnehaha Avenue and Lake Street in South Minneapolis. She had just returned from 10 years of living in Guatemala and southern Mexico; she still carried the voices of the Maya indigenous people with whom she lived. In those years, Teresa's poetry was heavy with vivid descriptions of the horror and bravery that she witnessed. As she worked at the resource center, Teresa lived the plight of the new immigrants. She felt a commitment to tell the stories of her people from Central America, Mexico, and those living in Minnesota.

Lupe Castillo identifies as a Xicana-Indigena from the Southern Lands and was born in El Valle, the Lower Rio Grande area of Texas. She has a deep connection to the borderlands as her birthplace and soul connection with her Abuelita. Her family traveled across the country with dreams of a better life, and at 4-years-old, Lupe's family joined her grandparents, the only Mexican family in the small town in rural Minnesota. With her lived experience of isolation and lack of visibility, she began journaling her truths and, in those truths, her voice came to light. Lupe's poems connect with ancestral knowledge, culture, and seeds of resistance. The feminist power she brings to her poetry magnifies her identity, intimacy, and the power of love, revolution, and struggle.

The vision for this collection stemmed from a 20th anniversary Palabristas event in September of 2022. Shortly after the celebration, Teresa and Lupe began conversations about collaborating on a book of poetry. They started collecting their poems and deciding on the thematic rhythm of the book. Aaron Johnson-Ortiz's artwork became an important addition to the collection with impactful visual images that depict the emotions and narratives in their poems. Finally, William Burleson, from Flexible Press, helped shape and transform this dream into reality. Bill supported the project every step of the way with suggestions and a blueprint on how to structure the book and offered them the opportunity to publish this collection.

In these pages, you will find poetry that will make you feel at home. In these stories, you will find the love of family, courage, bravery, pride, and dignity. These stories will take you from the Mexico-US borderlands to Minnesota to Central America and back again. These stories will welcome you and remind you of enjoying a cafesito while a friend share their life. We hope they will encourage you to be brave, show love and respect to your loved ones and honor those who have gone before you. May we all be brave and fight for our people and remember our roots are buried deep into Madre Tierra.

As we close, we're reminded that the waters in rivers, lakes, and oceans interconnect all of us as people who belong here and to all of America.

Poems By

Lupe Castillo

Identity

El Valle

The Rio Grande Valley (El Valle) feels like home to me,
even though I was raised in "Greater Minnesota."

Raised among the Midwest lands of soybeans, asparagus, and beets that needed to be harvested for the Midwest dinner tables.
Growing up I was never assumed to be Spanish, Espanola.

With my Indigena Mexica features, I always knew the blood in my veins was of our ancestors. I held my head up high knowing the lineage of our people are of the earth, celestial and spirit worlds.

Mis Bisabuelos, Abuelos, Ama y Apa, y mi angelita!
Your lives have taught me strength, survival and yes, even forgiveness.
I have learned to survive and thrive through the pain and trauma of the world without valuing our personhood.

These were just stepping stones to a bridge that brings me here today.
Poco a Poco/Little by Little
I make my way back to, El Valle,
as it feels like home to me.

You are my guidepost, from Minnesota to El Valle, I will always reach for you until I land on our ancestral lands.
Feet travel to the steps of my Abuelita's humble home, her being my destination.

I breathe the air and it feels alive, full of memories of Abuelita's loving care.
The Rio Grande Valley (El Valle) feels like home to me,

My body breathes,

My heart opens,

I walk in the footsteps of my ancestors as her door opens to welcome me home.

Identity

You Won't Remember Me

You won't remember me tomorrow,
I'm the Indigena you
        don't
                want
                      to see,
Do women who mirror your earth-colored skin
        remind you of whom
                you really are?
Our multiplicities making us
more whole.

I'm the hembra you are afraid of feeling
within your soul,
or know you never could,
        use your spiritual consciousness.
I am aware of my tonal, my essence,
        gaining awareness of my
ancient symbols and gifts.
Connecting the earth's elements to rituals creating
 alignment for familia y comunidad.

 I speak the language of our ancestors,
calling for protection

to surround my children.

I speak the broken Spanish
        you don't want to hear, as you use the "proper" Spanish.

I'm the copal, cumino, ancho spices and
flavors you don't recognize.
Memories of teachings from my Abuelita allow
healing from within.

Do you honor the journey your Abuelita
has sacrificed for you?
Do you buy into the self-hatred
that this world thrives/dies on?

I'm the blood in the veins of the women of Juarez,
 the disappeared, the forgotten.
Their voices can no longer be heard, over the
buzz of the factory machines.

Bodies cannot be seen
as they are left touched, but not loved.
Bodies left in the sun, but not warm.
Single shoes lay in the ravines of mud, symbols of unexpected captives.

Missing and Murdered Indigenous Women,
walk to their grandmothers house,
        never to be seen again.

DRESSES of RED, color of blood and also of honor,
h
    a
        n
           g
for each life as we search for her.
You refuse to see the beauty of our bronzed skin
    embraced by strength,
resistance, and survival.

We are the seeds of survival,
    Warriors of our familia's.
We are the promise for tomorrow,
    Teachers of our youth.

We are the elders of the future,
    Keepers of wisdom.
We are the spirits of our future,
    Protectors of our communities.

We will be remembered!
as we will walk in Courage.
We are remembered as our youth learn from our lessons and actions.
We are remembering to heal
our earth,
as we
WILL
HEAL!

Identity

Her-Story

Hermanidad, Abuelita/Madre/Hermana/Hija/Nieta,

Women Spirits/Spirit Women.

You will see her gathering with beautiful and powerful women who carry stories in their hearts.

These are the stories that bind us, the stories of us young and naive as we dream of greatness before we were told we were not great.

It takes time and awareness to undo what has at times been done to us. Take care of your heart and let your heart take care of you.

She will share stories of broken promises before she even knew that there could be such an act.

The stories of joy and life that carries us to
each other through the other side.

I feel your loss for words, at times the pain of remembering is too great to bear.

Hearing the release the chains on your tongue,

    so words can

        escape.

Writing will give you the key to unlock your stories and your life.

I hear the trembling of your heart as you courageously write, as you courageously remember the Forgotten.

You will see her sitting with you, as she tells you,
that you are enough,
that you are more than enough!

You will see her as I again reflect those words upon my soul.
As I share my story, weaving light paths between us to shine brightly, to shine boldly, to shine courageously, and to shine lovingly.

Shine upon those moments where Darkness rises and we write away our fears.
Together our voices bring our stories to life, and the witnessing of our stories allows our Spirits to rest.

This is Her Story,

This is Your Story,

THIS IS OUR STORY.

Familia

Mujeres In My Life...

Mi Abuelita, Reina de mi Corazón!

Our morning cafecitos, across the miles her,
minutes from the Rio Grande border and me,
hours from the Canadian/Minnesota border.
We talk about dancing.

A love of movement runs through our D.N.A.
She has the memories of dancing under the stars,
She shares that she would still dance if her body allowed her to dance,
sway and dance some more.

I will surprise her and take her to see her lifelong amigas, to dance, laugh, and share comida. Witnessing mujeres that share stories that I may never know, yet, I have a feeling I do.

I can imagine the stories between mi Reina and her Comadres are full of colorful memories both joyful and with sadness.

Micaela, who owned her life, found her love, and danced, until she was 90. She once said, you could write a poem about me, I said of course! I have written many poems about mi Reina!

I share poems with her about her, and she asks me "who is that poem about?" She does not see herself as I see her.
My poems are a mirror to her life.

She will see my life is a poem of her, of her resilience, of her love of music, dancing and Mexican Ballads. She shares stories of attending bailes with the Senior Center. Her smiles tell me she can still feel the music in her soul.

My Sunday's are a ceremony to her and to the womyn who give me strength and lift all our hopes to the sky!
Music fills the casita with Selena, Lila, Tish, Jenni, and Susana, along with other musical divas.

Prayers that mi Reina will still dance, when I see her again, creating space to see her, experience her life through her stories and voice.

Recent visits I am sitting next to her, sharing family history, stories, bits and pieces that can be remembered over worn photographs. She shares history about the women in the faded photographs.

Mujeres in her life, Ancestors in my life.
I speak about the Mujeres in my life to my grandchildren, sharing the legacy of resistance, survival and strength.

Mi Abuelita.

Familia

Drum Song

Mijo, Hombrecito,
Drum Beats,
    Heart Beats,
They are one
in the same
for you.

I stop and stand hearing the familiar drum beats,
As I hear your drumming, before I see you,
You have continued your drumming!

I hear our comunidad in your drumming,
I feel their prayers in each drum beat,
You instinctively, succinctly touch on the deer skin covered huehuetl.

I see the hearts of our warriors in your eyes, as you keep your pained strained arms on the drum beat as if the ancient ones depend upon you to guide their journeys home.
Drum Beats,
    Heart Beats,
They are one
in the same
for you.

Many hearts, many souls hear your drum and are re-quickened as they bring hearts back to their familias.

Sun rises upon your soul,
Souls rest upon sundown.

"Mama" you say to me,
"My spirit dreams keep drumming and I awake with new songs."
Heed these songs Mijo, it is the ancient ones that have gifted you
to bring the inherent rhythms of our raza to our
comunidad/communities hearts!
Drum Beats,
       Heart Beats,
They are one
 in the same,
for you.

Familia

Abuelo

Mi Abuelo, Mi Rey,

Sunday Football, I watch as you sit deep in thought.

I feel the distance between your world and my physical world,
as you are preparing to pass over to the spiritual world.
We talk about the game, and about family members who ask for their Abuelo.

I remind him he is loved,

    He is loved,

        He is LOVE.

I feel your heart heading back home, home to our celestial world to join, spirit to spirit with our ancestors.

I look at the Vikings sweatshirt laying upon the family Altor, remembering you recount the close calls, touchdowns, and flags, to me your Nieta who is at your side…

Not being a football fan, I watch the games just to enjoy the moment of being your Nieta. I never faltered in supporting "your Vikings team" as I passed you a beverage.

Your recipes shared are still treasured today. Salsa, with crimson red tomatoes, blazing green jalapeños and all the ingredients sizzling in the sarten/pan, are added to the molcajete.

I think about my grandparents and how isolating it was to have been to leave your homelands in the Rio Grande for a brighter future in the Midwest. The first family in the rural town where everything around you is unfamiliar and unfriendly.

Such a vast difference between El Valle and Minnesota. From desert heat to the frozen white capped fields of MinniSnowta.

I remind him he is loved,

    He is loved,

        He is LOVE!

Memories of you dancing with mi Abuelita, during house parties are known to be the highlight of all gatherings. Laughter, delicious foods, musical notes fill the home of which you are now saying your goodbyes to Grandchildren, Great-Grandchildren, Children and your beloved wife.

There's a sweet sweet spirit in this place. The song plays over and over as I help care for you, as you prepare to join mi Bis-abuelo's in the spirit world.

Your last goodbye was to Abuela,
Her face near yours to listen to the inaudible words to us, but to them, it was a complete language.

A language only shared and understood between the two of you.

I remind him he is loved,

    He is loved,

        He is LOVE!

Abuelo, I hold you close, SIEMPRE!

Familia

Your Memories Live In My Heart

Your memories live in my heart,
Fire burning, keeping us warm, singing to our ancestors to guide you home.

Your memories live in my heart,
For the loved ones to visit with us,
granting us moments.

Your memories live in my heart,
I act on loving those that I am committed to.
I want my dear hearts to know how much I adore them.

Giving thanks for her as she works to bring healing
to those that must stay here,
as they long for the spirits that have faded.

Your memories live in my heart,

As we search for Missing and Murdered Indigenous Women, the Women of Juarez, Water Protectors, Land Protectors, Prayer Warriors, we are them and they are us.

We must search for each of our Daughters, Aunties, Mothers, Grandmothers, Granddaughters, and bring their hearts home.

Home to us, Home to our families, Home to our Communities and most importantly,

HOME TO THEMSELVES!

Your memories live in my heart

Cañada
Aaron Johnson-Ortiz

Spiritual

Miracles Of Circles

Sacredness of creating and
cooking together as we
make miracles of circles.

The unscientifically valued
process of mujeristas
sharing ritual
in making tortillas
para familia y amigas
is transformational and healing.

Sharing memories as she sips on the glorious Nescafe.
At the age of 95, Nescafe cafesito is easy for her to make for herself.
Tortillas never taste the same
outside of my
Grandmother's kitchen.
Making miracles of circles as our
ancestors selected their
migratory pathways
for their people.
Travel based on the
alignment of
stars and sun beings.

Making miracles of circles creating foodways patterns
on the land.
Danza patterns following
ancient rituals of movement,
creating reclamation of our legacy.
Making miracles of circles
tortillas on the comal.
Hot slightly scorched
perfect circles.

Making miracles of circle
Remembering her hands as she
made the fresh tortillas de
mano y Corazón.
When I was younger,
I stand next to her during one of my visits;
as she works the masa rolling them out
and placing them
in my hands.
The gentle weight
of the dough,
eases the elasticity
of the masa.
Making Miracles of Circles with my Abuelita.

Spiritual

Dia De Los Muertos

Our family altor is filled with cempasuchil flowers that create the paths to guide our loved ones home, to be honored, and remembered.

Honoring my fourth born child who was only here for a short time, and losing parents in the last three years, and now mi Abuelita, the family Altor reflects their memories.

I deeply cherish the phone calls and the time shared with mi Reina/Abuelita.
Bearing witness in hearing my Mother's Mother as she is missing her daughter, my Ama.

In caring for Abuelita I want to make sure she is eating,
She has passed along the love for good food to me.
¿Qué estás comiendo Abuelita?

She is almost boastful as she believes the foods taste best in El Valle.
I believe it is because we are on our Southern Indigenous Lands.

She asks, Why are you in El Norte?
I know she means, Why are you not here? Arroz, tacos, frijoles, con salsita, I envision her eating these delicacies with warm tortillas de mano y corazón!

Placing photographs of beloved family members on our Altor, brings them closer, and opens the pathway home.
Selecting the foods and beverages each family member liked creates the familiar smells and tastes they enjoyed while living on the physical earth.

Abuelo's Vikings shirt and salsa,

Abuelas corn cake and arroz con leche,

Mi hijitas photo,

Tamales, y pan dulce for everyone,

Mezcal for the elders,

Candles for warmth,

Elements in the 4 directions, Earth and Sky,

and water for thirst.

We gather and share memories as we wait for our ancestors to honor us with their visit,

their teachings,

and their blessings,

DIA DE LOS MUERTOS

Spiritual

Ocotepec

Today, I share this solstice con los compañeros de la pueblo, Ocotepec with sincere hearts, different lives, similar visions, yet all with hearts reclaiming tradiciones, de los ancestros.

I see a church con viejito walls, crumbling stones, surrounded by black wrought iron gates, steeple strong, like my anima.
I hear, Yes mijita, our arms open to you,
it is our ancestors, calling my spirit,
 pulling on my corazón.

I almost doubled over with emotion, con dolor.
I feel the spirits of my ancestors.
Their voices lift me up and share their hopes for my tomorrows.
My path was carved for me before I was born.

Listen to our sacred songs,
Songs of our curanderas picking hierbas to cure our community.
Songs of our mothers singing to our babies.
Songs of our babies laughter healing our
Abuelita's/Grandmother's hearts.

Praying to the Maguey for honoring us as we create together.
With care, we accept the gift of Aguamiel to make medicine for our community.
Maguay seeds, the last flower, and Aguamiel are harvested and carefully placed under the light of the moon.
We sleep knowing our teachings will carry our visions
for future generations.

Seed saving,
Aguamiel harvesting,
Medicine making,
Solstice souls rest,
to return to the Maguay for the
the next day's ceremony.
 Ocotepec with sincere hearts, different lives, similar visions,
yet all with hearts reclaiming tradiciones,
de los ancestros.

Spiritual

Dia De La Virgen Guadalupe

Mi Reina, as we are speaking across the miles,
about what we are doing for the day,
I share with her that I am working on new poemas/cuentos.

My whole being is composed of poems about mi Abuelita. My
memories create the paths of water that carry me through every
hardship, and every pain to the other side.
The woman who showed me how to stand on my own,
Stand in my power,
Stand in my convictions,
Stand in allyship with others,
Stand in fierceness when speaking to injustice,
Reina Tonantzin earth colored skin ties us to the Indigenous beginnings
of all.
Grandson's first visit to La Virgin's site, and we walk along the path to
the Shrine of Guadalupe.
The church sits high on a hill, with a backdrop of a blue pearl sky.
We enter the church of blue stained glass
windows create prisms along the stone walls.

Blue glass candles lit with a prayer
        and at times, a plea.
We have our moment in lighting a candle,
        a lifetime of prayers, with our heartspeak.

Mi nieto/Grandson waits for me,
each of us keeping our hopes and dreams with
        Tonantzin-La Virgin de Guadalupe.
Tears stream uncontrollably,
Mi nieto/Grandson keeps close, as if
to stand guard over my teardrop prisms.

I am shaking as I say my silent prayer,
I'm here Abuelita, do you feel me?
Do you sense me calling,
        crying out your name??
llamando, calling, thinking of your spirit.

Until I speak with you again,
High on a hill,
        in a church of
blue glass prisms,
            shimmering slices of my
 broken heart,
casting light on stone walls.

Spiritual

Storms And Souls

Storms swirl, Souls storm

Hearts rage, Broken hearts

Streets fill, Blocked streets

Voices scream, Heed voices

No justice, No peace

Vision gone, Shared vision

March now, Must march

Feel pain, We feel

Womyn missing, Protect Womyn

Bring home, Ceremony bring

Call winds, Plants whisper

Burn copal, Copal messages

Drum songs, Sing drums

Prayers shared, Spirit prayers

Honor Elders, Respect honor

Food shared, Grow food

Open kitchen, Welcome open

Singing medicine, Elders singing

Spirits guide, Guiding Spirit

Fire burning, keeping us warm

Singing ancestors, guide you home

Cempasuchil flowers, show the pathway home

Copal smoke, opens prayers

Me, praying

I'm here, you're there

Souls and Spirits

Storms and Souls

Spiritual

Suenos

Mi Reina,
I dreamt of you, when you were here with us
in this physical world, we spoke of the time when you
would pass into the city of Angels.
My heart will lay next to you,
looking over to you, to see you and ask
Lita, are we together yet?
You've known me so well,
Both you and I have pierced the stories that others have placed on us.
We broke the thin veil of transparent mesmerizing

rainbow Colored prisms,
To give birth to ourselves,
Mi Reina,

Are we there yet?
Your one year is here,
today, 12/24/24
this morning at daybreak.
I await the rise of the Sun, el Sol
to bring light to the dark,
Lita, are we there yet?

The memories of you bring warmth to the cold of this Minnesota morning.
The hours before this particular morning,
I awaken upon the hour.
Each minute the loss quickens.
Christmas Eve morning,
one year ago,
        your heart no longer beats.
We will no longer hear
each other's laughter
over coffee,
across the 1496 miles between us.
We will no longer share the happenings of your life,
who has visited you, or the dish I am working on.

Your laughter was soul healing.
Another red full flower blooming this morning,
 and I know it's you sending me beauty, and renewal.

The bright red petals of the hibiscus flower provide life after death.
I acknowledge the gift as I do with all your regalitos
you send throughout the day, along my walks,
during difficult times,
 you are always here with me.

Upon the minute, the ritual begins,
the offering I place in my hands,
long strands of hair.

I honor you and send peace for your spirit.
I strengthen my will to continue my healing path.
Your resilience has been my firefly of light and hope.

I look to you and ask,
Lita, are we there yet?
Rest in Paz y Amor

Insignia Nacional
Aaron Johnson-Ortiz

Activism

Zapatistas

Jan 1st, 1994, they showed themselves. Indigenous, Voiceless, now Represent and are truth-tellers.

In the jungles of Chiapas our jente had been organizing around mesa's for 10 years before showing themselves.

Zapatistas standing strong in 7 towns read their declaration. Zapatista's rise as they would rather die from a bullet than continue watching our jente die!

They were/are the voice for the voiceless.
Sharing the energia of all who wanted a better life,
and to live daily without fear,

Stand strong for Human Rights
Through wearing the "Zapatista Masks" they were/are seen!
We must be Seen and Heard!

Through their Stance, they were/are Seen.
Through their Palabras, they were/are Heard
Together we will Work/Fight for Justice

Together we will Write/Speak for Humanity
Together we will Live/Aspire for our familia
Mujer Zapatista will live, teach
and build for our Future Generations.

Our young men stand strong in "Harmony"
Protecting our community
Protecting our alliances across man made borders

The huehuetl/drum brings the community together for the next Mesa
We bring our voice, our heart and fuerza for justicia!

This Mejicanita was "Forged for This!"

Activism

Vamos a Luchar

Vamos a luchar por la raza,
Vamos a luchar por la familia,
Vamos a luchar por la justicia,

You say as a mujer I can fight by supporting you…
But, your weight bears down on my body taking the breath out of me slowly with each exhale.
You put your hands on our bodies and expect
us not to yell and take

       your souls.

You say as a mujer I can fight by standing by your side,
But, when you have respected positions within the community, you send us away with no insurance to take care of the new generations!

You say as a mujer I can fight by never questioning you in public, that we can take care of it behind the doors of our casitas, but not in front of the other's, the Güero.

But, we never speak in our casitas, and the silence is felt. You say as a mujer I can fight by having constant meals prepared and not only prepared, but bien sabroso!
You never kiss the hands of the abuelita's
that bring comida to nourish your soul.

You say as a mujer I can bear your children to have
¡Un Raza Unida con beliefs en familia!
But, your heart not appreciating or understanding the
blood shed in this sacred ceremony, and it is not you or your kind that I
want to bear my children.

Si, voy a luchar,
Fight for la raza, la familia, la justicia to see women who are strong, who
can love in our own way

If we don't fight for our children,
If we don't fight for our rights,
If we don't teach our children that they are worth our bloodshed,
so that they can walk in dignity, so they can walk in honor,
we have nothing!

They will walk with honor,
dignity and
with eyes ahead!

Mexica Tiahui!

Activism

Warriors

For the loved ones we lost in the struggle towards justice,

Let your heart rest on mine and softly land

For those fighting against injustice,

Let your heart rest on mine and softly land

For those feeling the loneliness,

Let your heart rest on mine and softly land

For those with addictions trying to begin each day,

Let your heart rest on mine and softly land

For those with babies who only grant us moments of time,

Let your heart rest on mine and softly land

For those who hold the hands of people we love, leave

Let your heart rest on mine and softly land

For those who offer justice by showing the truth,

Let your heart rest on mine and softly land

For those who continue to see humanity,

Let your heart rest on mine and softly land

Cruz-y-Ficcion
Aaron Johnson-Ortiz

Activism

Witness

I witness stories of survival,
stories of people not realizing
that they have survived.

I bear witness to their pain,
and also to their will to
live again, and AGAIN.

You will also find me
whispering to the winds,
my hopes and dreams
for my children.

I hope they are happy, healthy
and fulfilled,
in this world that
does not necessarily want happiness for them.
Our children are warriors!

I have my own luchas,
and I find paz in the
quiet of my heart.
This is where,
       I
              will
                      find
                              me.

Retrato
Aaron Johnson-Ortiz

Love

El Mar

Dreams of sand sprinkled feet,
sun kissed bodies,
sipping ice cold fresh fruit juices
poured into plastic bags,
straws are free.

Dinners of street corner taquitos,
deep sun sets,
rays reaching beyond
our horizons.

Ocean waves surround me,
water spans forever creating a universe of azul,
only to do it all over again…

Love

Giving Thanks

Giving thanks I ponder the act of giving,
as my amiga, hermana,
writes from the sands of an Island.
I feel her distance and heavy heart.

Giving thanks I feel the
 gratitude of the ones
we have here on earth,
our loved ones,
 praying they are well,
happy, & healthy.

Giving thanks,
I act on loving those that I am
indebted to, committed to.

I want my dear hearts
to know and feel
how much I adore them!

Giving thanks, the elders speak
to the taking of lives on her
homeland.

The despair of losing
community members
is felt in her words.

Giving thanks for her
as she works to bring healing to those
that must stay here on this earth.

Giving thanks as they long for
those spirits that have faded
and traveled on their way home.

Giving thanks,
Praying our ancestors will
guide their way home.

Giving thanks for our Elders wisdom that
keeps our hearts strong.

Giving thanks for Indigenous Peoples
as we hear their lessons.

Giving thanks as we walk within their footprints.
They have created the path for us to follow.

Giving thanks for our ancestors resistance,
that we are still here and will remain here.

Giving thanks and honor to our people.
We must bring our loved ones home.
Giving thanks for our children learning our danza ceremonies.
Giving thanks for dreams with messages
from our loved ones to share.

Giving thanks that we have the
opportunity to transform,
Giving thanks for the transformations.

Earth

Madre Tierra

Heart to hand,
Hand to Earth,
Harvest to heal.

Children laughing,
Elders singing,
Mother's humming.

Gardeners tending,
Farmers sowing,
Roots furrowing.

The canopy of trees gifts us with coolness,
in the bright blazing sun.
Heat-filled days are lightened with the love of family.
The Mississippi runs as a travel path
from North to South.
My people traveled the lands,
South to North.

My hands placed the seeds,
in the bed of tierra.
Nurtured by our mother's hands,
Sun lifts the roots to the surface.
As we continue to place seeds in the earth,

Laughing,
Singing,
Humming,
Tending,
Sowing,
Harvesting,

Mother Earth has, and is,
trying to teach us.
We must understand,
extraction only takes from us!

Flora and fauna,
will feed our families and communities,
as we are from the Earth.

Born of water and blood,
we reach for the Sky.
as plants reach for the Sun/Sol.

Hungry for nourishment,
Land stewards feed our world and
create the world, to pass on
to our next seven generations.

We give birth to
Water protectors and Earth protectors.
 In the gardens we listen as plants communicate
 their language to each other.
I look up from my prayers and see
Elders teaching our youth,
people preparing food.

Babies teaching us patience,
Together we plant, sow, and harvest,
our ancestors gifts of seeds.

I honor our seed keepers,
carrying our seeds within the hems of skirts,
and trenzas of our hair.

Seeds to protect
and continue planting.

Heart to hand,
Hand to Earth,
Harvest to heal.

Earth

Elders

Children of my Children,
My hair is greying,
My steps are slowing.

With new birth's, new bonds, and new beginnings,
My words are softer,
And my heart is stronger,

You may see me as your Great Grandmother, your Abuelita.
But you must remember Our Earth,
Tonantzin Tlali is our true Mother.

To her we must care and take care,
Not by yourselves, but arm in arm, gently, bring
and teach others to care for our MOTHER EARTH.

Mother Earth's zone is greying,
Landscapes are slowing, sounds are softer,
And her core is weary.

Let us carry forward together,
Side by side,
Spirit with resistance.

Sharing our visions,
Speaking our truths.
Caring for our Madre Tierra.
Tonantzin Tlali is our true Mother.

Earth

Healing Is...

Ending Missing and Murdered Indigenous Women!

Ending Brown Children in cages!

Ending shooting of our community members in their homes and streets!

Ending broken promises of education!

Ending the genocide for our people!

Listening to Truth Tellers and we heed!

Healing broken threads of familia bonds

Answered prayers that all can live with dignity!

Seeing the humanity in each other!

Artists as healers in our communities!

Ceremonies are held sacred with Danza and Song!

This is Healing...

Inframundo 2
Aaron Johnson-Ortiz

Poems By

Teresa Ortiz

Identity

Espejos
(Spanish version)

Somos espejos

Que reflejan nuestros rostros color tierra

Que es tu rostro

Que soy yo, tu, nosotros

Miranos, somos, aqui estamos

Espejos de nuestras memorias

Pinturas de patrias ancestrales

Espejos en danzas de aves mariposas

Que vuelan en parvadas,

Van y vienen, anidan, se quedan, se regresan,

Van y vienen,

Aqui estan!

Danzas de recuerdos olvidados que se hacen vida

Con tambores, ritmos, pasos

Espejos en palabras que cantan nuestras voces

Que gritan nuestras voces, que hacen eco,

Que recuerdan vidas ya olvidadas

Vidas ignoradas que renacen en canciones esparcidas por el viento

En lenguas nuestras, tuyas, antiguas, inventadas

Espejos que retratan mil colores del cielo, del agua,

Reflejados en el agua cristalina de estos lagos

Los azules, grises, verdes,

Turquesas como piedra, verde selva

Color barro de la tierra

Amaneceres de fuego

Rojos incandescentes, rosas violetas

Espejo el conejo de la luna blanca

Espejo la noche negra

Espejo somos como la sangre del rio

Que conecta nuestras venas

Sangre del rio

Que conecta el norte de estas aguas

Con los mares del sur y a nuestras tierras

Somos espejos

Aqui estamos

Somos las raíces de árboles
Sumergidos bien profundo

De aqui somos
De aquí y de allá de nuestra tierra

Espejo mi rostro en tu espejo
Miranos, aqui estamos

Somos indios, mexicas, mayas, Ojibwa,
Somos negros, mestizos,
Americanos somos,
Mexicanos, caribeños, centroamericanos,
Andinos, sureños, Latinoamericanos,
Chicanos, Norte Americanos

Miranos,
Aqui estamos,
De aqui somos

Espejos nuestros rostros
Que retratan nuestras vidas

Espejos
Somos

Espejos
(English version)

We are mirrors

Reflecting our earth colored faces

It is your face

It is I, you

It is us.

Look at us!

We are! We exist! We are here!

Mirrors are our memories

paintings of ancestral lands.

Mirrors are the dances of butterfly/birds

flying in flocks.

When they arrive and when they fly away;

when they stay and when they nest;

when they stop in mid-air

and when they come back.

Look at them! Here they are!

Mirrors are the dances of our forgotten memories;

dances that come alive with drums, rhythm, steps.

Mirrors are the words we sing with collective voices.
The words that we yell aloud with collective voices.
words that bring back forgotten lives,
ignored lives,
lives that are reborn by songs broadcasted through the wind,
in languages that are yours, mine,
ancient, invented.

Mirrors are the paintings,
murals colored with the thousand colors of the sky,
reflected on the crystalline waters of these lakes:
in blues, grays,
turquoise like precious stones, rain-forest green,
brick-colored red like earth,
sunrises made of fire,
incandescent reds, violet roses.

A mirror is the rabbit inside the white moon.
A mirror is the blackest of nights.

We are mirrors.
We are the blood of this river
pumping into our veins.

Blood of this river connecting the Northern waters
of this land
with the Southern seas
and with our homelands.

We are the roots of trees dug deep inside the soil.
We are from here,
from here and from there, from our homelands.
Mirror is my face inside your mirror.
Look at us! We are here!

We are indigenous
Mexica, Maya, Ojibwa, Dakota.
We are Black, mestizos.
We are American.
Mexican, Caribbean, Central American,
Andean Surenos, Latino Americanos,
Northerners, Chicanos.

Look at us! We are here! We are from here!
Mirrors are our faces
portraits of our lives.

Mirrors, we are!
Espejos, somos.

Familia

Papi Mingo Tells The Story Of Espiridion Salazar

My father had a talent for making us laugh
Short round figure in a business suit
Bald head covered with a fancy hat
Tilted to the left side
Wrinkly slits of eyes that disappeared when he smiled.

My father spun stories with no ending
Rhythm rapping / strings of words
Nonsense rhymes / Old-folks proverbs
Made up legends from ancient lands
The names of towns in his railroad train route.
And the story of a trickster:
Espiridión Salazar.

My mother
Standing by the window
Soaking sunlight like a cat
A book always in her hand
From my mother
I learned about my past
The lessons of my elders

The history of my family and my homeland
A wonderful storyteller
She weaved tales of passion
Struggle, triumph and loss:

Love letters pinned to a lamppost
Roses for the opposition candidate
Caballos para la Revolución
Los bisabuelos texanos who moved south
When the borders also moved
The adventures of el abuelo
Tears rolling down her cheeks
While listening to a Mexican waltz

And the night the lion roared
So that my father could declare his love

I grew up to my father's nonsense rhymes
I grew up to my mother's tales of love.
I grew up to my great aunt's eyewitness accounts
Of courage / violence
In Pancho Villa's war

I grew up listening to the music of my home:
Stories of bravery in Mexican Corridos from the borderlands
Ancient legends in Spanish Romanzas from across the sea
Teachings of social justice in CRI-CRI children's songs
Sones, huapangos, jaranas, rancheras:
Native and African tales in rhythmic melodic sounds
The beauty of Indian cadences / Filtered into our tongue

Like genetic engravings
These stories stuck to my soul
From them I learned
The rhythm and the rhyme
The magic of the words
From them I learned
The meanings of life
What is just and what is wrong
The history of our people
The lessons of our past
And to never ever trust a man like
Espiridion Salazar.

Familia

Papi Mingo's Rhyme
(The original in Spanish):

No hay conque me debes, que te debo,

Que te firmo un vale,

Que esto y que lo otro,

Que fue y que vino,

Que chocolate con cuchara y café con tenedor.

Espiridion Salazar,

enciéndete una vela y apágate un cerillo.

Para mi no estaba muerto.

Calavera se volvió.

Cuenta la vieja leyenda polaca que allá en Polonia

Cuando se proclamaba su independencia en el año 14

De la Era Cristiana,

    San Eligio,

        Salamanca y

            San Pedro del Cobre.

Papi Mingo's Rhyme (Translation in English):

There is nothing that you owe me

not at all that I owe you.

I would not sign you a bill.

There is none of this, nor that.

Sip your cocoa out of a spoon,

stir your coffee with a fork.

Espiridion Salazar:

Light a candle, blow a match.

For me he was not dead,

he just became a skull.

According to the old Polish legend

In the year 14 of the Christian Era,

When Poland was proclaiming its independence…

    San Eligio,

        Salamanca and

            San Pedro del Cobre.

Familia

Crazy Comandante

Ten days before you came
I ate tacos at home and went for a walk
on a country dirt road.
Our dog Eric was running ahead of me,
prairie wind blowing / messing up his mane.

You told me you were coming. I felt it in my bones.
But no.
I had to wait ten days for you to come.
And then you were so tiny when you finally came,
that I had to wait another three months
to bring you home.

That was only the beginning…

They say:
That there is a beginning and an end to every story,
the middle is everything that happens in between.

We were living at the farm back then,
in the plains of Minnesota-
when you were a child with brother and sister
and you liked to run and dance.
The swallows used to fly, surfing on the prairie wind,
from the porch of our cabin to the weeping willow
in the bottoms by the creek.

As a man, when you lived in the colonial house
in southern Mexico, you had a parakeet,
who used to be your brother's before yours.
She went everywhere with you perched upon your shoulder,
until she flew away, and forever left.

Remember when you fell face-down and sank into the mud
in La Selva, in the town of Realidad?
You were reaching to shake the hand
of the tiny horseman Zapatista Comandante.
With crooked smile upon your face, you tripped,
falling full-bodied into the sinking mud,
disappearing from sight.

Lifting yourself up without hesitation,

you ran towards the waiting bus,

dripping mud all over / all around you,

dirtying seats and compañeros,

staining the tile floor of the sidewalk café

where we stopped to eat quesadillas

in the town of Comitán, on our way back home.

You were always marching for justice - a fist up high,

talking to everyone around, always ready with a hug,

a smile,

truly convinced that you could change the world.

You were always so good at dancing salsa,

you had the rhythm in your soul,

the perfect moves.

One day you stopped, and said:

"You guys don't get it, do you?"

And you were probably right, because for us,

when there was an invasion inside you

everything changed in our whole world.

For some strange reason it made me think

of that time in history

when Tenochtitlan fell to the foreign invader,

when an ancient civilization disappeared into the sinking mud

And everything changed in the entire world.

Everything changed in the entire world.

A dark cloud sat over the weeping willow,

on a cold winter night.

I held your hand, I said,

"Everybody loves you. Did you know?"

You smiled.

A winged archangel flew out of the bedroom,

when you closed your eyes.

I saw you then, crazy comandante.

You disappeared into the mud, you flew.

Dancing like a crooked king,

like the wind you smiled,

you danced.

It happens that when autumn comes

trees dress up fancy clothes of crimson velvet and jeweled gold.

Exhausted drunken leaves fall into the ground after the party,

snow covers them up to sleep when winter comes,

and in the spring the leaves are gone.

Part of the earth they have become.

Part of the earth they have become.

I see you now this spring, crazy comandante,

I've seen you every day, from now, till then.

I see you dancing with the prairie wind.

I see you dancing with the prairie wind.

To the memory of my son,
Gabriel Dominic Johnson-Ortiz (7/16/1980-1/17/2015)

Rezo
Aaron Johnson-Ortiz

Earth

Shaokatan

There is a time of day in the prairie
when the wind stops,
and the babes in the nest
open their mouths wide
to better catch some air.

All day my ears have been used to
the roaring noise,
like waves breaking at sea.
My body used to the constant rhythm of
everything around me.
To the tightness of my skin.

But then, there is that time of day
when everything is still.
The grass stops its waving movement
blades reaching towards the light.
The branches in distant trees do not sway.
The hills look like photographs on postcards.
There is a muggy odor coming out of the earth.

This is the time of day in the
summer prairie
when the heat rises and dampens my eyes
waking up feelings long gone.

The memories come tumbling down
like weeds on a dirt road,
like tears rolling down my face,
as I sit watching my life go by
in the prairie
and the cattle goes on grazing by the ditch.
So still.
 It is but a few minutes or hours
or seconds.
And it is gone. The wind returns.
It dries up my skin.

The swallows surf on the air

as they sing,

as they catch insects for their young.

The blue of dawn colors the fields

in pale tones of velvet.

I am at peace, now that the gentle breeze

cools memories.

And as the sun goes down

and the sky turns red,

The wind gains speed.

 In the prairie, the world is

rushed again.

The stillness is no more.

Earth

The Mississippi Saved Me

Thank you trees for giving me your shade.
As I look up towards the sky, I see you.
Your branches forming a canopy are like an embrace,
like a loving umbrella of protection.

Thank you sun for giving me your light.
For shining your brightness into my soul,
for giving me your warmth.

Thank you cool air, thank you wind
for the freshness on my skin,
for making me shiver and tremble,
for the calm feeling in my spirit.

Thank you rain for getting me wet.
Cool raindrops, sacred water to cleanse my body.
Thank you…

As I walk, as I cross the Lake Street bridge going west
from Saint Paul to Minneapolis,
a little boy, maybe three years old, runs towards me.
He is laughing, wearing a bright red and orange t-shirt,

arms wide open, as if embracing the wind,

legs kicking as he runs, next to his father, who is walking by his side.

I laugh. I smile as I pass them.

The father talks to me in a foreign accent like mine.

He is wearing an incongruous, oversized, tie-dyed t-shirt,

and a bandana covering his head.

A scribbled sign written with chalk on the banister

gives me directions:

this way to Minneapolis, this way to Saint Paul.

Other signs,

written with chalk on this same banister on recent months

explained to passers-by the importance of peace,

of revolution,

that BLACK LIVES MATTER,

that oppression is wrong.

The Mississippi is under my feet,

under the bridge as I walk west.

I stop at the first corner of Minneapolis Lake Street

to buy me a coffee.

I sit at a table outdoors.

People are congregating at the restaurant next door

to the coffee shop.

It's amazing how soon people started to come out

back into the world

after the long months of confinement.
A grandmother plays with her granddaughter
next to my table.
They giggle and climb on the benches,
jumping up and down.

My intention had been to walk towards the river,
but it starts to rain and I decide to head back home,
walking with a smile on my lips,
wet under the rain, happy,
thinking that the world is a beautiful place.

These long, long months I walked.
The Mississippi saved me.
The river saved me these long, long months of confinement.
Minnesota saved me.
Saint Paul and Minneapolis saved me.

My neighborhood saved me.
The flowers on my neighbors gardens saved me:
the aroma, the colors, the beauty saved me;
the trees, the red-gold color of autumn trees,
the falling leaves, the golden light and
sunny, chilly days of autumn saved me.
The tender, new, light yellow-green leaves of early spring,
the freshness of the wind in spring,
saved me.

The greatness of bright flowering, blooming, upon trees
in a symphony of pinks and reds, upon trees
saved me.

Even the lazy days of summer,
the humid, hot, lazy days of summer
when the entire world seems to be taking a nap,
even summer saved me.
Even the frigid days of winter,
subzero temperatures, nasty weather,
nature painted white, snow and ice.
Even the cold frozen winter,
long nights, short days of winter saved me.

Nature, mother earth, the outdoors,
whatever you want to call it saved me.
The world out there saved me
from the long months of confinement.
It helped me survive. It helped me to be sane!
Cooped up in my small place, long hours in front of the computer,
no real human interaction,
worrying about friends and relatives sick,
being stressed out.

Every day, rain or sun, snow or ice,
I walked.
I walked to the Mississippi

one foot in front of the other,

face covered with mask,

breathing in, breathing out.

I sat next to the river, in front of the water

every day.

The water ran away by me,

moved south to my land. Slowly.

The wind caressed my skin. The sun came out every day.

People walked by me.

They talked, walked, ran, and biked.

Dogs went by. Children.

The world was alive by the river

The river saved me.

It whispered to me: "It is going to be alright"

And it was.

And it is.

Activism

Resistance

Don't be afraid, my mother said,
You come from a family of revolutionaries

You come from a long line of warriors.
Fighters who resisted the destruction of our civilization.
The destruction of cities, palaces and buildings,
our ancient culture, our music, our art.

Our ancestors, I tell you, they dared to build again.
Our ancestors stood up against the aggressors,
Adapting to new circumstances,
peacefully, but not quietly they fought.
    They resisted.
They rebuilt our culture again and again
    Always anew
Always changing it to create new art, music, architecture.
new, but ancient at the same time,
always remembering our ancient roots and true values.

You think this attack is new?
    They call us names.
They attack us, dismiss us, humiliate us.

They murder us
They steal our children away.

This is not new, I tell you.
Have you forgotten your own history?
    Let me say it again:
We come from a family of warriors, fighters, survivors,
      resistors.
These are our people. This is who we are. Don't you forget.
They killed us again and again,
But we did not die. We became light.

We were seeds that grew into flowers.
We bloomed. We grew. We became art and culture.
And music and food. Architecture.
Because we know how to work, to build, to create.
To care for each other. To love.

Don't be afraid, I tell you:
We are flashes of light that illuminate the darkness of the night.
    We can resist!

Activism

Drove Around Wisconsin Roads

Drove around Wisconsin roads
idyllic pastures, knee high corn.
Drove around the five of us
the wrong way for seven turns.
Stopping first at country church,
a rural farm / a farm house.

To blond tan people singing in church.
To golden children playing on grass so tall.
Idyllic pastures
knee high corn.

Drove for miles just to get there
to perfect picture town
to building green like fields
to red/white/blue star spangled banner
Flying up above.
To police headquarters / city hall
Library / county jail.
To Hartford,
Heartland,
Hard-land,
USA

Walked into wall-to-wall carpeted air-conditioned room,
as a dozen silver heads turned around towards us.
Squinted sky-blue eyes gave dirty looks
held their breaths:

Los indeseables have arrived

The ones they never see /
The ones they talk about
(the dark ones)
The ones they want to
Eliminate / Obliterate
Criminalize / Illegalize / Deport
Send us back to where we came from

Remind us always: You are not one of us

"It's disgusting, just disgusting"
a woman stood up to say.
Complained about bilingual ballots,
about telephone lines where
Spanish is spoken when you touch a one

"American should be the only language in our land,"
she said.
Demanded more troops at the border
and a bigger wall.

Sylvia, sitting next to me,
was fuming while holding her breath.
Whispering, trying to understand
"Que dijeron? What is it that they said?"

Ana,
so quiet behind me,
I could feel her pain.

The Congressman, presiding in front of us,
sitting in an armchair like a king,
shaking his head in agreement to the racist talk.
He is the one
who wrote the infamous bill
that caused millions of immigrants all over the country
to hit the streets in protest,
that moved the masses in affirmation of their rights.
A wake-up call of a movement that will not stop until
we are heard,
until there is real change.

And there we were:

Traveled from so far away

just to see him,

to argue our point,

        the five of us.

We raised our hand in protest

raised our voice / shook our fingers

accused the accusers

pointed out the obvious, the unfairness of it all

That, what they didn't want to know

Senor Congresista,

What do you know about anything,

comfortably sitting in your armchair?

Who do you think cleans the halls

of government buildings like this one?

City halls / libraries / police stations

of all the Hartford, Heartland, USAs?

Who adorns the beautiful gardens in city parks?

Who fixes the roof in your house?

Senor Congresista,

How long do we have to wait?

For justice, fairness, equality in Hartford, Heartland,

USA?

How long do we have to wait?

To be treated like the citizens that you claim to represent?

And there we were:

In this Midwestern town.

Beautiful park with flowers,

flags of many nations,

kitsch folklore in the corner craft shop,

with art and crafts of the lands that we are from,

Spicy food from our cultures in the restaurants downtown.

Polluted river running under a bridge

Polluted water streaming under the bridge

And we want to know:

Who will clean the city of Hartford, Hartland,

USA?

When all the "indeseables" are sent back to where we came from?

Activism

Dignidad

"They thought they could kill us, they didn't know we were seeds."

We stood by the lake's shore in a circle
Holding each other's hands, embracing each other's hearts
The silence broken by the women's wailing
Sadness and rage are prayers in the form of protest

Just the day before the farmers' bodies still lay on the ground
Today,
Flowers, candles, incense, crosses covered the grass.
A year after this,
At this same site,
Where once an army barracks had been
There would be a planted field,
Corn growing among the crosses

Once I walked on a path on the cornfield
Milpa planted on the mountainside fed by
Human remains buried beneath our steps
Overshadowed by the ruins of a firebombed church up ahead.
This is how it is in here

Walking downhill into the ravine
There's a shrine on a mesa,
Just a flat concrete slab
Decorated with hanging banderitas de papel.

A few years ago, two days before Christmas,
Forty five people were assassinated while praying.
Their bodies are buried under the shrine.
Behind the altar's cross, there are mountains,
Where coffee grows
Harvested by the survivors.
Cups of sacred brown blood are drank all over the world

So that you may see us, we covered our faces" (Zapatistas)

Their land was stolen,
Natural resources were destroyed,
Water sources depleted
They have been exploited, put down
History denied,
Genocide.

People who have been in this land before the world was round
Fighting in
A millennial struggle for resistance,
For the earth, for human rights
An army of farmers who will not give up
Until things are made right

> *"We were reborn as giants, we are now fragments of light that impede the darkness of the night."*

"Welcome to my home, your home,
The earth, a place to dance"
He said with covered face
A smile sheltered behind black cloth
"Welcome to this revolution of seeds
That with love multiplies"

Warriors quietly working, fighting
With power, genius, culture,

Dignidad

Activism

On The Road To Palenque

So long it takes for the morning to wake up
In the mountains of the Mexican Southeast

The clouds come down to the earth
To kiss the corn
Before the sun decides
To travel around this side of the hills
Towards the valley
In order to burn the fog

I become obsessed
With taking photos with my cell phone
As we ride downhill in the tour van
On our way to Palenque
As the sun comes out
As the morning brakes
As my daughter and her friend sleep
On the van seats behind me

I am obsessed with catching in quick shots
The beauty of this moment in this land

Yet it is such a task

To portray in images the exact green color of the fields,

The tenuous grey-blue color of the sky,

The yosh-blue turquoise sacred color

Painted on sacred Maya crosses

Placed standing by the sides of roads,

The mountains trying to reach the sun,

The corn taller than I,

The cacophony of multicolor designs

Upon clothes and homes and churches,

The horses running free on fields as if they belonged

only to themselves,

The turkeys with colored ribbons tied to their feathers

For owners to recognize,

The smiles on people's faces

Those

That you can only see

When looking into their eyes

Because bandanas are covering their mouths

Chiapas has a hold on me

So many years I lived in this land
So many years ago it was
And I always come back

Even back then, it was quite a task,
To convey in words to foreign visitors
The dignity and the joy of valiant people
To explain complex concepts
Like culture, survival,
Resistance, revolution,
And low intensity war

So hard it was to recognize, even to myself,
My own feelings:
The tears from my eyes,
The passion of the soul,
The jumping of the heart,
The excitement of struggle,
The certainty that a better world was coming,
The friends / the laughs,
The sadness afterwards,
The rage when peaceful people were murdered,
The pain / the grief

And the dark hole
From where I thought
I would never be able to crawl out.

"Those were intense years,
Weren't they?"
A friend reminded me just yesterday
She works with women in the villages
Like we both did back then
She talked about the changes in the communities
I talked about the changes in the United States.
We both seemed to agree
That the more we struggle
The more it feels as if we are pushed back

I think of all of this
As I travel to Palenque
I think about her words:
"But we cannot lose hope."
I think about this beautiful sunrise in the Chiapas highlands

I think,
That it just takes a long time
For the morning to wake up

Spiritual

Eclipse

When Zotz the bat
opens up his enormous black wings
the sky turns grey and misty

Red shadows cover the mountains
as if a thousand bats
flapping their wings
flying all-together up above
covered the sky

The shadows come slowly,
moving on the hills
the way the wind moves the corn on the fields
Like waves

A golden ring appears in the sky.
A magical signal
a signal from the gods appears in the sky.
Shining all around it.
Covering the clouds with a golden glow.
A gold ring with precious stones around it.
Covering the clouds with a silver glow

Covering the clouds with a golden glow.
And the day
becomes the darkness of the night
And the Sun
Is there no more

When the sky darkens
the animals sing.
They howl to the midday dark sun
the golden ring disappearing sun

An ancient music
Maya music
Monotonous, magical music
Earth shaking music
Howl-like sounding music
like the hoot of the owls sounding music.
The ooh ooh
song of the caracol shell
covers the air as the animals sing

The children bang on the turtle-shell drums,
they shake their rattles, they whistle and yell
to scare the bat away, to make it go away

The unborn children, inside their mothers' bellies,
do somersaults and hide.
They cover their heads with their tiny arms.
They cover their eyes with their tiny hands
and hide,
deep inside their mother's bellies.
While the abuelas, the midwives, the suegras,
cover the women with shawls, with ponchos
to protect the child inside

The men run up the church tower.
They ring the bells
to warn the townspeople.
They ring the bells
to scare the bat away

On the mountains,
deep inside the jungle,
the shamans meet
      to light candela,
to burn copal,
to look into the sky
for the prophecy of the golden ring
in the darkness,

of a new day coming:
"After the darkness of Xibalba
A shining light will arise
El Sexto Sol se levantará"

At the top of the highest mountain
at the top of the highest temple
of the Kingdom of the Cakchikel,
that's where we sit

"Mirá!"
Our eyes are covered with the golden glow.
Our eyes are blinded with the golden light.

Until Zotz flies away
And the day becomes the daylight
Again

Inframundo
Aaron Johnson-Ortiz

Spiritual

Medallas

As a young woman in my twenties
I carried four medals on my chest.
Like a decorated general
I had four medals that gave me strength.

My first medal was for a brother,
who shot a bullet and died.
He was many years my elder,
a captain in the army.
(I loved him so)
I was seventeen years old.

The second medal
was for the bullets falling from the sky.
Shattering a woman's ear, killing hundreds more.
With us hiding in a dark basement,
listening to the shooting outdoors.
Watching shadows of soldiers chasing students,
holding them under pouring rain with their pants down

The third medal was for the river's sand.
Germinated / Expelled from my womb.
Waking up to a sharp pain,
to a white shadow against a white wall.
The sun outside, blinding my eyes.

The fourth medal was for a broken nose,
in a dark alley on a winter night.
Scarlett blood on my sky-blue coat.
Yelling in Spanish for somebody to help me.
(Nobody came. Nobody understood.)
Running away from there as fast as I could.

I am an old woman now.
How many words would I need,
to tell you about my life?

I had a happy childhood.
If ever there was such a thing as that.
A brother who taught me to dance,
another who taught me baseball,
a third one who was my best friend,
a fourth one who told me I was a princess
and then died.

A mother who narrated the stories of my homeland.
A father who recited rhymes in rap.
A house full of animals and plants.

My earliest memory:
The aroma of roasting coffee
Filtering in through our apartment's windows in the back
My father's advice:
"Everything you own, you could lose,
But your life is yours to live until the day you die."

I am an old woman now.
How many medals have I earned
throughout this long life?

The biggest medal was for a son, my first born,
a warrior, a rebel,
whom I so much loved and then lost.

Medals for other loved ones lost,
for lost possessions and lost relationships

I have worked in rebel territory.
I have taught people to read and write.
I have crossed so many borders so many times.
I am a citizen of two worlds.

I have a daughter and a son.
Whom I adore.
I got a talent or two, I got a job.
I have friends who care about me.
Every day I see the sun.

I can survive anything,
Because these medals don't weigh me down
These medals make me brave.
These medals make me strong.

Mal Augurio
Aaron Johnson Ortiz

Spiritual

A Poem Spoken

A poem thought
is the wind softly whispering into your ear,
a repetition of syllables,
sing-song verses dancing inside your brain,
ideas of phrases that keep coming back and back,
as you walk, as you go around your day,
with verses that will not go away until they become a melody, a rhyme.

A poem thought
is a rhythmic song that gives you joy,
a love song that is only for you alone to love,
a song that slowly, methodically, takes form.
It is the poem that is never just out there,
for the world to read, to listen, to enjoy.

A poem written
starts only as markings on the paper,
with corrections and scratching,
with care for the grammar, for the rhythm of the lines.
It is the frustration with the words you choose,
the throwing of the paper away into the trash,
ripping it into pieces every other time.

ALMA Y CORAZÓN: WRITING IN THE RHYTHM OF LIFE

Never to be happy with the way it sounds
(maybe because paper doesn't make a sound
other than the sound of crumbling it and ripping it apart)

A poem written
is the symbols that appear on the screen,
the tic-tac on the keyboard under your fingers tap,
a copy and paste of moving lines up and down,
and down and up again,
revising and re-reading it and
feeling it's just not yet right,
     until it is,
          or almost is.

But a poem spoken:
A poem spoken is an illness in your stomach,
goosebumps on your skin,
a dizzy exhilarating feeling
of adrenaline jumping at the heart.
It is being naked in front of everyone,
telling your truths and lies for the whole world to listen,
(even when they don't listen, or maybe barely listen).

A poem spoken

is like shouting on the mountain,

or more it is like shouting at the farmers' market,

in the middle of a street, a stadium full of people,

a pub / a bar / a coffee shop, the park,

or reading out loud at a library, a living room in somebody's house.

Sometimes, a poem spoken,

is reading as people walk by,

doing their shopping, dancing, talking.

But sometimes,

it is reading to some people,

      some, enough,

who are listening to the verses you recite.

And at that moment that is all you care about.

A poem spoken

is the shaking of your arm with paper in-hand,

it is not remembering the words to say,

and then you do,

      you shout!

It is the movement of your hips, like dancing,

a talking with your hands,

a fist up in the air,
      a serious look, a smile,
a silence at the end.

A poem spoken
is a song without an orchestra behind you.
It is only a voice,
      your voice,
telling the world your truths, your lies,
shouting into the mountains
words thrown out to the wind,

    for them to fly!

Paloma blanca paloma negra
Aaron Johnson Ortiz

Acknowledgments

I dedicate this poetry book to my children, grandchildren, and great-grandchildren, as I write my truths and speak words of wisdom, power, and resistance. Your courage and resiliency comes through the veins of our ancestors as you guide the next part of your journey.

I am deeply grateful to my partner Britt Howell for her undying support, encouragement, and assistance in editing various poems shared in this poetry book. She bears witness to our shared poetry journey, our "writing in the rhythm of life."

Mil gracias to community artists/poets/activists Dr. Jessica Lopez Lyman and Maria Isa Perez-Vega who provide hope and inspiration for our future!

Giving thanks for the poets that shared time while visiting Minnesota, Gloria Anzuldua, June Jordan, Ana Castillo, Cherríe Moraga, Sandra Cisneros, among others that have encouraged me to put pen to paper and inspired me to fearlessly write my truths.

Alma y Corazon: Writing in the Rhythm of Life has been a journey of love, loss, pain, and healing. I walk to honor my ancestors and my familia, I write to share history and stories that intersect our lives.

I would also like to thank Aaron Johnson-Ortiz for the artistic drawings that are embedded in the book and vigilance in creating space to celebrate LatinE artists in the Midwest and across the Americas.

I want to thank Flexible Press for patience and steadfastness in the journey of publishing our dreams and stories of resistance, survival, and healing.

— *Lupe Castillo*

I feel great gratitude to the many people who helped in the realization of this book, a dream of many years. These poems, written here, were the result of years of love from my family and my friends, and the inspiration from my ancestors and my community. Gracias to my beloved children Carmen Maya and Aaron Marley and to my son in Heaven, Gabriel, for your support and love. And to Aaron, thank you also for the beautiful art drawings that accompany this book. Throughout my writing life, I have had the support and encouragement of many friends in my community and the writing community. I have belonged to several writing groups where the poets and writers have read and revised my poems and have helped me to develop as a writer. Gracias to all the members of my writing group, to my Palabrista compas, to the women poets. Also gracias to my familia de origen, to my ancestors, my parents and brothers, for inheriting a love for art and poetry, history and identity. Gracias to my comunidad in Mexico and Minnesota from whom I have learned so much! In the development of this poetry book it has been wonderful and exciting to work with my companera/amiga, Lupe Castillo.

Working with Lupe has been a fascinating experience of meeting regularly and working on our poems together in an amicable spirit of collaboration. And great fun! Thank you for everybody who encouraged us, supported us and worked with us every part of the journey to be able to get this book ready for publication.

— *Teresa Ortiz*

About the Artists

Lupe Castillo (La Poetress)

Lupe, Texas born, Minnesota raised, shares the experience of Southern roots with Midwest musings. Being one of only a few Latina families in her childhood community offers the lens of resistance, survival, and thriving.

Lupe is the creator of HeartSpeaks: "Voces de Cultura/Voices of Culture Healing & Writing Circles" and is a self-identified XicanaIndigena from the Southern lands. As a Culture Bearer, HeartSpeaks provides activated collaborations in writing and spoken word artistry. Lupe guides participants in writing about their connections to family, community, and cultural identity. Workshops are held in community groups, high schools, and universities.

Lupe's recent poetry is documented in the Northside Green *Our Urban Canopy* coloring book, the University of Minnesota's Chicano Latino Studies history archives, and in *Boundless—The Anthology of the Rio Grande Valley International Poetry Festival 2019*.

In 2024 Lupe began workshops that facilitate and elevate the lives of Latino poets and writers through the "Places We Call Home" poetry workshops with The Minnesota Humanities Center.

Lupe is a co-founding member of Palabristas—LatinE Writers/Poetry group.

"I write what I am willing to live up to, and possess,

my truths. Let us all have the Will to Write and Write to Right the injustices of our existence."

Teresa Ortiz

A Mexican writer, poet, storyteller, and spoken-word artist, Teresa writes in Spanish and English to honor her ancestors and her loved ones. Born and raised in Mexico City and northern Mexico, Teresa has been a resident of Minnesota since the 1970s, living in the Twin Cities and in rural southwestern Minnesota, and for several years in Chiapas (Mexico) and Guatemala (Central America). Her writing depicts the sacred places where she has lived, the amazing people who have touched her life, the beauty of community, the energy of revolution, and the memories and inheritance from ancestors and loved ones. Her past published work has include her book: *Never Again a World Without Us: Voices of Maya Women from Chiapas Mexico* (EPICA 2001); short stories "El Rio" in *Lake Street Stories* (Flexible Press 2018) and "The Children's Mountain," in *Home* (Flexible Press 2019), and several poems published in chapbooks and literary journals. She is a member of the Latino spoken word collective, Palabristas, and has presented at many events throughout the Twin Cities; and she is presently a member of a collective of fiction writers.

In this anthology, Teresa aims to reflect on the beauty around our lives, the sacredness in nature and mother earth, the magic of Latino culture and indigenous spirituality, the power of history in our own lives, and the love of family and community. In these stories, Teresa reflects on experiences that take us from Central America to Minnesota, with feelings, descriptions, and images that turn us into protagonists of history.

Aaron Johnson-Ortiz

Aaron Johnson-Ortiz is a Mexican, Mexican-American, and "Mexi-Sotan" cultural organizer, arts advocate, and award-winning muralist based in Saint Paul, Minnesota. His "Workers United In Struggle" mural was named the 2018 "Best Mural" in the Twin Cities by City Pages. Aaron holds a Masters in Fine Arts from the University of Michigan in Ann Arbor, Michigan. Additionally, Aaron is the Executive Director of (Neo)Muralismos de México, a Minnesota-based Mexican and Latino arts nonprofit organization, and the Founder of the Minnesota Latino Museum project, NMM's initiative to develop the first permanent museum focused on Mexican and Latino arts and culture in Minnesota. Aaron has 20 years experience working in the fields of community organizing, arts leadership, public art practice, and cultural advocacy. Aaron is also a founding member of the Mexican Cultural Arts Alliance, the only national alliance of Mexican-led arts organizations and cultural centers.

www.ingramcontent.com/pod-product-compliance
Lightning Source LLC
LaVergne TN
LVHW041612070526
838199LV00052B/3114